Fixed Star

Fixed Star

Suzanne Frischkorn

JACKLEG PRESS

JackLeg Press
www.jacklegpress.org

Copyright © 2022 by Suzanne Frischkorn. Published
2022 by JackLeg Press. All rights reserved.
Printed in the United States of America.

ISBN: 978-1737513476

Library of Congress Control Number: 9781737513476

Cover design: Richard Every
Cover art: *Mystic Scribbles 9*, Reb Livingston

Other Books by Suzanne Frischkorn

Girl on a Bridge
Lit Windowpane

Chapbooks

American Flamingo
Exhale
Red Paper Flower
Spring Tide
The Tactile Sense

Praise for *Fixed Star*

Elegant, clear-eyed, and restless, Suzanne Frischkorn's poems seek and illuminate the frayed hyphens fastening us to family, to the world. Her searching is psychologically rich, transformative: an iridescent interiority spirals outward to touch what sustains it, what divides it. Structurally brilliant, alive with lyrical thinking and observations, *Fixed Star* is ample proof of Frischkorn's poetic gifts. In her hands, language is light.

—Eduardo C. Corral, author of *Guillotine*

In Suzanne Frischkorn's intoxicating *Fixed Star*, content and form mirror and echo each other, twin and twine. From the opening line in the first of a sequence of sonnets that generates the book's architecture, "Birth cleaved me in half," we learn that the subject is separation, from first language, landscape, and heritage, a loss, a violence, a thievery carried by and negotiated within the body, which becomes, itself, a translation. So what, then, can poetry be? In Frischkorn's hands, it is— well—everything. It is the cry and the answering cry, the body's disappearance and revolution, history and tangled myth and the site of self-creation, honoring the fragments while languaging them into something greater, more songful than a whole. Much of the book's authority emerges from Frischkorn's formal virtuosity.

And then there are the voices she braids into the poems. Transtromer and Plath. Keats and John Cage. Shakespeare and Olga Guillot. They are lyric companions on a perilous road that takes her to Lorca, from whom she learns that "Leaving is difficult. Sometimes / to stay, invites death." *Fixed Star* cannot be reduced to anything but itself. I am in genuine awe.

—Diane Seuss, author of *frank: sonnets*

Contents

Primera

Segunda

Primera

Cuban Polymita

Birth cleaved me in half—
the sea I grew legs in
now a dissonance,
a fixed star—the Atlantic

where I summer cannot diminish
the dichotomy. This figurine
with its sash cinched by gold leaf,
its delicate arm grafted with glue.

It's the din of fiesta
I hear on the boardwalk
that green button of memory.
An ear[ring]

tucked into an envelope
found in a bureau with the scarves.

II

Found in a bureau with the scarves
an imprint of identity
a single gold ball stud —
evidence of cultural piercing.

A lace dress. A first language.
All myths once we move north.
Washed on shore we lost our heritage.
Sometimes it happens

when you're standing —
watch yourself.
Perhaps it's as effortless as drifting.
The soft light of a streetlamp

on a November morning
taking the edge off the stars.

My Body as a Communist Country

Its betrayal totalitarian —
skin dry as parchment

      lit by the slightest brush.
The scent in our

sheets sets off chimes,
a measure until you

      return.
The minutes I swallow whole.

Castro, you've nothing in Cuba like my desire.

      My body's capitalism,
greedy. It's a slow-jam

in a darkened room
keeping time with a DJ.

      Its lyric, *the blue light of aging shadows*

desire's waking. Ten years from now
      we'll wonder at this

my body's exacting power
      brooking no opposition.

How Do You Say Orange?

After we left Hialeah for the Poconos,
My parents only used Spanish to curse

   maricón, puta negra.

The same language spoken
by the maids at Mount Airy Lodge

where my father worked
        as Head of Housekeeping.

The day he introduced Dora, the maid
he slept with, I could not respond.

        The scent of Cohibas,
a recipe for black bean soup

and how to roll the r in *naranja.*
That's all the Cuban my father gave me.

III

Taking the edge off the stars
is like unmasking a lizard.
How do we know something
true if we don't see it?

The glare of a gleam —
a dazzling trick.
The eye must only trust
what is tarnished. Watch

someone be lost for awhile
and then translate without moving.
What does it mean to disappear?
To lose the little sea inside you?

It was a grand procession
on the grandest of avenues.

IV

On the grandest of avenues
how could we lose
our way to the vacant lot?
I am sorry

for not being truly sorry.
Trunk upon trunk
ficus trees build themselves out.
Crossing a wide boulevard

under these clouds
I pursue the life given to me.
This sheet of water
covering the ground.

The winter sets its teeth.
Nothing given us to keep is lost.

My Body as The Tropicana Nightclub, 1952

My body's Arcos de Cristal lined
   in licentious points of light.

It's the crème de la crème and the güempa.
   It's a legendary simmer.

      ¡Mami estás matandome!

It's Latin Jazz syncopation.
      The trumpets hold its melody.

      Roulette, Baccarat, Craps, 21—
my body, the flashy casino of beauty.

It's the showgirl girdled in orchids
between sets, and it's her sequins' shimmer.

Its bolero—*lie to me, tell me you love
      me, even if I know you don't.*

Pool

Desire your name is Miami,
stirred with a snip of sugarcane,
crushed mint, Bacardi, and sunning
yourself by the Biltmore pool. No, Miami,
I sip mojitos, while I am stroked by the eyes
of the cabana boy—he is heady
with a cocktail of bikini and tropical oil. "You know
how when you go to Little Italy it's all Chinese now?
That's how Little Havana is, but with South Americans."
We decided to skip it and drink
mojitos by the pool. "Cubans?
They're everywhere," says the concierge
with a Cuban wave of his hand.
"Maybe, you'll see some signs with Spanish writing…"
We drank mojitos by the side of the pool,
while I was desired, and realized
I don't desire you, Miami.
Miami, you are not what I recalled
yet, only within you do I feel desired.

Papaya

In *Blow,* a scene with Penélope
Cruz was so like a mirror
                    I said, *Oh. I'm Latina.*

                    *

I didn't know the papaya tree
                    scars on its trunk as its fruit

ripens and falls. Or of its pale
                    blooms, its fecund seeds, its carnival hue.

                    *

If you speak quickly I will understand if I don't
try to understand my first language. You must

understand it was stolen—
legend, song, all of it
                    a fading stain by firing squad.

V

Nothing given us to keep is lost.
The stud earring, the green button—
memory knows no walls.
Qué bonita. How strange,

how foreign—the creak
and jangle of the burros' reins.
I am quoting here and elsewhere
from the translation, objects appear

dim and blur on the right side.
The invention of memory—a seamless
indivisible act. Altered street signs
in a world full of traffic signs.

A scintillation around letters indecipherable
unable to identify what we're seeing.

VI

Unable to identify what we're seeing
when entering the sphere of another
life. *The coup, to my judgment*
is already lost. The tension between

desire and domesticity is a familiar one.
No one knows yet whether the romance
will ripen into love and profits. When
Fidel took his bow, the crowd

made a hero-welcoming noise.
And who is that at the door on this dark night?
Once you delve into the question of sex
the strings begin to twitch and the smallest

gesture needs to be reckoned with.
Here, as elsewhere, people have departed.

My Body Translated

It is the dark,

dusty ground that gives

       to tobacco its aroma and flavor.

       The hills confine its valleys,

rich in vegetation and exotic orchids.

Plateaus and mountains increase in height

       from the west to the east.

Its formation throughout the western coast,

       unusual eroded limestone.

A sacred place, my ample valley,

and it holds disregard

       for the wooded distance.

What It Means to be Cuban, Hyphenated

It means I'm on a journey —

                        Is the soil blood red, or brick red?

To witness   miles of tobacco's green waves.

Yes, I know,   no yearning for the island,

or talk about a Mango tree in the backyard (Carol City).

What about burrs in the grass pricking my feet?

                Graffiti?   My Cuban sitter built
a tiled shrine to Mary,   my only mother.

                 I sat   at her feet   for days.

What it means to be Cuban

        hyphenated?   I don't know —

My father's from Cuba. I'm American.

He wanted me to learn one language really well.

VII

Here, as elsewhere, people have departed.
Mi querido, I think of our afternoons,
that spent light, and I wish
I could live underwater—

my skin would absorb the sea.
In the chamber of memory
whatever it was, they had lost it now.
What killed them isn't known.

By the time we reached the property
night had fallen. Topiary animals—
the dolphin rears on its tail,
the crocodile leaps towards a window.

He took careful note of what needed repair
where water collected and timbers rotted.

VIII

Where water collected and timbers rotted…
"I must be gone and live or stay and die."
So, which is it: tears or no tears?
The Wagnerians take their seats.

You see things that only you can see.
The wind sings to you—beautiful, but dark.
I wanted to make poverty elegant.
He was sensitive to intrusions of sound—

quiet and loneliness, tendrils of melody.
I tried to become someone else for awhile
Only to discover that he, too, was me.
Witness a dance performance: We don't

believe in a world of the haves, the have-nots.
It's an odd form of capitalism.

My Body as a Revolution

Its propaganda tucked
        inside a push-up bra.

Nascent

The quest brought its own interstellar medium in the end. She was matter between stars in a galaxy of stars. The yoked constellations—Capitalist and Communist—rang bright on her skin. *Fidel, is it cold in Cuba?* She is nascent, still, because her body is here and she is not. A numinous zephyr lily of love – cloistral and cognizant – laminated to each star. *Suzanita* is but one stria here. The lathe is the sinew and the cloche, terracotta. *Entiendo?* The Royal Palms have closed up shop.

Palm Tree Cento

This is not something I've just learned
there was a sphere, with dark patches like mountains

and I swear by this stolen image
you should listen to what they are hinting.

Over there evil and good actually have faces.
How I would like to believe in tenderness

to know that light falls and fills, often without
our knowing. I am not speaking of rose windows.

Here after a meager diet of horizon is some scenery:
All the leaves stuck out their tongues.

IX

It's an odd form of capitalism.
In the stands the man with his hands
on his hips and his head tilted back
searches for answers. *People, man,*

they love hurting people.
Whatever these women do
like others, they want to see the world.
"The money change happened so fast,

nobody had time to think."
And while I could end there
I have no desire to.
I need a history more complete.

So I continue with my father's story,
making up details as I go along.

X

Making up details as I go along
I held my hands up to the generals.
I walked around investigating:
the endless star, an empty net, the fish

trapped inside the wind.
The first night was wonderful—
adrift amid the remnants.
In the empty house I hear the sea.

The boats were manned by brothers,
uncles, cousins, blood ties, a bond
love can twist. All the years by the sea
taught her every definition of blue.

There was a lot of lechery and disorder.
And I am queen on that island.

Black Spring

In March 2003 Normando Hernández González was among seventy-five Cuban journalists who were arrested in what became known as the Black Spring. This poem was found in interviews on his experiences.

I held my breath under the bed
curled like a knot against the wall.
They searched cars.
They searched everywhere.
Searched everything.
       A small incandescent bulb lit

twenty-four hours a day.
I always talked. If I had the desire
to speak, I spoke.
My only sunlight hours
Monday through Friday at noon.
       All seven of us remained in solidarity.

We began our hunger
strike on the 13th of August.
They took everything.
Including the mattress from the bed.
All they left me was my underwear.
       The cell was completely boarded up—

a small crack at the top of the door.
If I stood on five books

I could look out into the prison.
There was not an inch of me without
a mosquito bite. Small, red, bumps on every,
          every, every, every, every part of my body.

I never could sleep in that cell.
To get through something like this
you think about your family.
I believe that was my wife's saddest experience.

She doesn't even like to speak of it—
          of when they let her see me.

I didn't stand up when they did head counts.
I wouldn't dress in prisoner's clothes.
I never addressed any guard or official by rank.
I was beaten with rubber sticks.
In Cuba even to breathe is illegal.
          To breathe! If you breathe the air

and, while taking it in,
you don't praise the government,
you are being unlawful.
It's as if the sky and the earth are going
to come together and crush you.
          And no one will notice it's happening.

Leaving prison was like being born
with experience. Everything I do is motivated

by love. There are remnants that remain.
I would like to forget,
but, unfortunately, I cannot forget.
        And this is how it is.

XI

And I am queen on that island—
"I am and will always be
a Mariana in combat."
'Dear captain: with urgency

I am answering your note
be assured, I repeat, we will
strictly observe the truce.'
At that moment we were all

Cubans. This is what we call
The War of the Entire People.
How are they going to defeat
our people? How are they going

to defeat our revolution?
Each woman knows what to do.

XII

Each woman knows what to do.
Darkling I listen;
and, for many a time I have been
half in love with easeful Death.

It follows that we are best off
when we understand things least.
I can see the walls and arches
the columns and statues

and the lonely towers of our ancestors
but I don't see the glory.
 The question is what I'm doing
with my life, but all she said

aloud was, "This is where I'm from."
Birth cleaved me in half—

Segunda

Exilio

Conch shell pink, this sky echoes an ocean; a song weighted with pearls and sea glass. Mercedes, what did you make of Miami? Did it taste like sunlight on your wrist? White mariposa replaced by ribbon orchid. Jasmine, a scent of dreams. And flamenco? *Las Guajiras?* Castanets cast on the ground. Your granddaughter will seek you in a hundred mirrors. In Castile, in Cuba, she'll twine a history with silver thread. The ocean will rise up to whisper in her ear.

La Dama Azul

The Blue Lady, Jagua Castle, Cienfuegos, Cuba 1745

This castle, *Nuestra Señora de los Angeles,* is nothing more than a sleepless sentinel. Restless, I note each wave of the Spanish Main and pace this fortress along its high walls. Only in the chapel do I discover solace. What is the nature of obsession? It is desire; desire for the return of your galleon, *mi amor, mi corazón.* I am almost invisible with longing. All that is left of me: a shadow of raw blue silk. This morning a young officer was found with his broken sword beside him, a skull, and a blue cloak. The guards claim I drove him mad.

When My Granddaughter Asks

About the woman in Cuba
      I will tell her that each night

she released a cascade of black
      from its trap of pins until it settled

at the small of her back, and that is why she birthed

eleven children; but will be unable
      to explain her penchant for O's—

Ofelia, Othelma, Onieda,
      or need for R's—

Rosselio, Renaldo, Rafael.
      I will not say she abandoned my father

and his siblings without wisdom
      because on her way out

she left Oneida's hair scattered
      on the plank floor kitchen,

a five-finger lesson imprinted on my aunt's cheek.
That will teach you to feed a man without a job.

Math

You spend all day coaxing your students

to trust that x = y, and to share your joy

in a clean angle, yet your wife fails

you—her eyes shut to your formulas—

although she admires the simple math

of fractions. Tonight she serves a dish

from Cuba—a country with too much sugar—

pernil y arroz congrí . She rubs in a paste of garlic,

vinegar and oregano, remembers the first

meal, the tiny kitchen, how she calculated

so you would come back for more.

Early evening and the sun cuts the horizon.

The sky's hue echoes an ocean—

conch shell pink. Your plate in the oven, still warm.

What I Know of Sugarcane

*In Cuba the annual sugarcane harvest begins when
the rural population bids farewell to the macheteros.*

The stalk, made of segments called joints, each joint

    a node and an internode;

here leaf attaches to stalk,

    here, find buds, find root primordia.

Despedida de los Macheteros! O national pride.

    O solidarity. Here, a leaf scar

discovered when a leaf drops.

    Farewell machete wielders: 44,000 men

in rubber boots, straw hats, gloves.

    Buds: miniature stalks with miniature leaves.

Cuidado macheteros, struck stems spray hot syrup

    on the skin. One bud presents

on each node; one side of the stalk

to the other. Men side by side between

dense blades. Loose rows of primordia exhibit

dark centers, caps, light halos.

Here, macheteros bear stems on their backs.

Spanish

Speak its measured notes, recall the year long in paper,
the cargo ship's scent, a single rolling wave, the sailors—
tick them off your fingers, melodious. Listen, you can not
even name his brothers, and abuela's becomes a hymn,
Mercedes, Mercedes, Mercedes, a song to weed the garden
by, *Mercedes*—this is how we lose the language, how we
lose ourselves to myth, to legend, and how you find me,
with regrets only.

Once I Dove into the Caribbean Sea

Isla de Cozumel, '93

Cuba, its tide strove to draw me towards you and failed. I departed with a smooth shell and wisps of surrogate sky. How cool marble caressed my bare soles, how heat plied my skin bronze. Not until I slide the silver bracelets from my wrist will the strains of your shore ebb.

[36]

Spain at Leisure

Madrid

Cibeles drawn by wet lions. Mother
to three hundred ten trees.

Toledo

El Greco fools them all. Bougainvillea
spills down the granite hill.

Cordoba

Light's austere kiss brushes stairs—marble &
jasper flood the dark mosque.

Seville

Andalusian heat is flamenco red—
staccato etched on skin.

Granada

The verse citadel, nightingale's thrown notes
   ghost Sacromonte's caves.

Mijas

The hibiscus village reigns in mountains—
   white glistens, sol's dry heat.

Málaga

Feria littered, strung and lit—doorway
  Picassos tilt today.

Torremolinos

Graffiti catenates every white wall—
  bougainvillea currents.

Jasper

Oleander divides the highway like a rill, its blossoms spill their wan scent. We pass sunflower fields scorched by government light, and power line poles wearing large brown hats—no, not hats, stork nests. Listen to wind cut by wing. The way to Cordoba, *mi hijo*, is to follow the silver leaf of an olive tree as it drifts and loops along arid soil. First go to the sea, its bed of soft stones an alchemy for sorrow, its salt like baptism. Here, sunshine sends you to bed, pink oleander whisper the formula for everlasting life, and hope is forever caught in the almond tree. Jasper's opaque hues stain your skin; it's the myth you carry home.

Letra

I discovered Cuba chiseled in Retiro Parque.
Glimpsed Cuba second-hand, and Canadian.
Cuba in picture books, its myths tangled—
paper cigar rings, cigar box treasure.

Cuba, I will come to liberate you, I promised
and toasted "Cuba Libre!" with some Costa
Rican ladies, they laughed and laughed
and laughed, "That was funny," they said.

On the terrazzo—drank café con leche, took
dawn with Spanish sky. (I have yet to meet
a flamingo I didn't like and still the stork
evades me.) In Cuba, right now, someone conducts

a symphony of furtive braiding for a tourist.
She'll leave before the last braid is half-done.

Tourist

She'll leave before the last braid is half-done
and recall a store closed for her business,
the Nike articles she stripped off her skin
and the confectioners' sugar beaches.

Santiago, Havana? You don't remember
yet, the sting of her vacation chases you
home like an errant wasp. A constant hum
in either ear. She spoke of Cubans as some

speak of children, how sweet and how
desperate. "That was a stupid thing I did,
going to someone's home for braids." She
means the scent of fear overcame

the stench of poverty, it touched her white skin.
A moment longer... it may not have rubbed off.

To the City I May Not Enter

I sing to my beloved Cuba... —traditional letra

Cienfuegos, pearl with the luster of a hundred fires, I
swallow you and taste your heat; the scent of white
mariposa its flue: pure and rebellious. A woman in a blue
dress caresses my nape and wings traverse to kiss my ear.
Where is José Martí, hero of Cuba? Where is his white
rose? O to see a hundred fires burn among your thick
stalks. Bay water beads on my heart. Light, bright as a
stone. *Mi Perla del Sur, Mi Linda Ciudad del Mar.* Your
palms render the rhythms of sun and gale even now as
contradaza fills my mouth.

Andalucía

A moment longer... it may not have rubbed off
the bougainvillea stain, its wine blossom. Rough
is the face of Serrania De Ron, and rough
the sand that spills from your palm. Darker

than expected, night over the Mediterranean Sea.
Strange to you these hot stars. White like Mijas,
and their ascent as hard. Had you known
would you still complete the journey? *No habla*

espanol, habla inglés, por favor? Qué hora es?
Time, we are speaking of time, how long
it takes a stain to set, a flower to blossom —
more than a morning? The acanto inspired

columns. And nothing you promise will
coax the palomas to follow you home.

Isla Cerralvo

I pursue the women before me to a desert island.
        The path skewed and scant.

The women left behind small songs—
        De la Cisneros, Hughes, Velozo,

LeGrande, Navarena—born by oceans.

               *

Two islands, from Cuba I've been exiled.

The other deserted, its sea mired in fishing
        boats; its history steeped in coral reef.

Camagüey, Cuba

—legends gathered by rain, collected in *tinajones*, white lake reflections, plains and mangroves. That rooster of Morón, *el guapo!* Antonio, toss her, toss her in the air and catch her, not the first girl to trust you, yet the last. Seafarers, rebels, men who roam, all the silver coins of love—sing your death's song, its notes the breeze on a nape, its tale of lost things.

Seville

Coax the palomas to follow you home
with a one-two beat, conga as if the last
moment had arrived, your percussion pulse
at its end. Rhythm gets you everywhere—

your hips most. Flamenco's staccato
beat brands your skin, Seville
dares the moon to dance with stars.
The love letter hidden in your pocket

from where the palm tree grows, Suzanita,
read it again, smooth its creases—
Guantanamera, guajira Guantanamera—
your navigator, and your compass.

Green, how I love you, green. Under the gypsy moon,
things are looking at you and you cannot look at them.

Granada

Things are looking at you and you cannot look at them,
lavender daisy, alone in a green sea, if you must drown
it is best to be lavender and alone. Here, in the General
Life gardens, morning glories bloom en masse. A visitor

wonders how exile fell on Moors, harbingers of water's
secrets, they who carved verses on their walls. You lose
yourself, or perhaps, wish to. Late summer garden
you have duende too. Leaving is difficult. Sometimes

to stay, invites death. I am speaking of the firing squad,
of having café with a friend on Monday, and learning
of his death on Tuesday. Come and see the blood
in the streets. I came to the source, seeking the shape

of my eye, my nose—I passed as a native, and at last
found a way home. I discovered Cuba in Retiro Parque.

About the Author

Suzanne Frischkorn is a Cuban-American poet. In addition to *Fixed Star*, she is the author of *Girl on a Bridge*, *Lit Windowpane*, (both from Main Street Rag Press) and five chapbooks. She is the recipient of The Aldrich Poetry Award for her chapbook *Spring Tide*, selected by Mary Oliver, an Emerging Writers Fellowship from the Writer's Center for her book *Lit Windowpane*, and an Individual Artist Fellowship from the Connecticut Commission on Culture & Tourism. She is an Editor for *$ -Poetry is Currency* and serves on the *Terrain.org* Editorial Board.

Notes

"Cuban Polymita IV"
Lines 11-13 are a variation of lines from Howard
Nermerov's "The Pond."

"Cuban Polyimata - VII"
Italics are variations of language borrowed from Cristina
Garcia's *Dreaming in Cuban*.

"Cuban Polymita- VIII "
Line 2, quotes Romeo, *Romeo & Juliet*, Shakespeare.
Line 7, quote attributed to John Cage, *Searching for
Silence*, by Alex Ross (New Yorker, October 4, 2010)
Lines 10 and 11 are from Stephen Dunn's poem,
Discrepancies.

"Cuban Polymita - X"
Lines 4 & 5 are variations of language borrowed from
Pablo Neruda's poem, *Enigmas*.
Lines 13 & 14 are from *Ninth Elegy: The Antagonists* by
Muriel Rukeyser.

"Cuban Polymita - XI"
Quote attributed to Brigadier General Teté Puebla,
*Marianas in Combat – The Mariana Grajales Women's
Platoon 1956-1958* (Pathfinder, 2003).

Lines 4 - 7 Excerpt of letter to Captain Batista from Commander of "Ciro Redondo" July 22, 1958, *Marianas in Combat – The Mariana Grajales Women's Platoon 1956-1958* (Pathfinder, 2003).

"Cuban Polymita - XII"
Lines 2 - 4 are from the Keats poem "Ode to a Nightingale."
Lines 7 - 10 are a variation on lines from the poem "To Italy," by Gaiacomo Leoparidi.

"Palm Tree Cento" Sources: Zbigniew Herbert, Nichita Stanescu, Bella Ahkmadulina, Andrei Voznesensky, Tomas Transtromer, Sylvia Plath, Theodore Roetheke, Richard Wilbur, and Elizabeth Bishop.

"Black Spring," is a text collage made of González's answers to interview questions in the book "The Madrid Conversations" Uno Press, 2012.

In "My Body as the Tropicana Nightclub, 1952" The bolero lyric is from Olga Guillot's signature bolero, "Mienteme" ("Lie to Me").

"Papaya" is for Dulce Menendez.

In "Seville," 'From where the palm tree grows,' is a line from Jose Marti's, *Versos Sencillos*. The last two lines are a variation on lines from Federico García Lorca's, *Romance Sonámbulo*.

In "Granada," 'Things are looking at you and you cannot look at them,' is a variation of a line from Federico García Lorca's, *Romance Sonámbulo*. 'Come and see the blood in the streets,' is from Pablo Neruda's, *I'm Explaining a Few Things*.

Acknowledgments

Heartfelt thanks go to Eduardo C. Corral, and Diane
Seuss for their generosity and kindness, to Hannah Craig
and Steven D. Schroeder for their insights,
encouragement, and friendship, to Reb Livingston for
gracing this book with her artwork, to Francisco Aragón,
Simmons Buntin, Rigoberto González, Cynthia
Huntington, and Dulce Menendez for their support
along the way, to the Connecticut Commission on
Culture & Tourism for the Individual Artist Fellowship
that made the writing of these poems possible, to the
wonderful team at JackLeg Press, especially to Richard
Every, Jennifer Harris, and Simone Muench for their
careful attention to this collection. And to my husband,
Jim, always. TJ, Jack, and Emily this one's for you—te
quiero.

I am grateful to the Connecticut Commission on Culture
& Tourism for an Individual Artist Fellowship that made
the writing of these poems possible.

Many thanks to the editors of the following publications
were these poems first appeared:

Avatar Review, "Spanish," "What I Know of Sugarcane,"
    "Camagüey, Cuba"

Barn Owl Review, "Nascent"

Copper Nickel, "My Body as a Communist Country"

Indiana Review's Latina & Latino Writers Issue, "Exilio"

MiPOeasias' Cuban-American Issue, "Letra" "What it Means to be Cuban, Hyphenated"

MiPoesias, "Pool"

New Zoo Poetry Review, "Math"

North American Review, "My Body as the Tropicana Nightclub, 1952"

Paterson Literary Review, "How Do You Say Orange?" Honorable Mention Allen Ginsberg Awards

Pebble Lake Review, "Cuban Polymita, "VI," "VII," "VIII," "IX," "X," "XI," "XII" and "My Body Translated"

Printer's Devil Review, "When My Granddaughter Asks"

Puerto del Sol, "Cuban Polymita, "I", "II", "III", "IV," and "V"

Silk Road, "To the City I May Not Enter," "La Dama Azul"

Saw Palm: Florida Literature & Art 10ᵗʰ Anniversary Issue: Florida-Cuba Connection, "Black Spring"

Anthologies

50/50 Words & Images (Goss: 183, 2010): "Papaya"

Some of these poems also appeared in the chapbook, *American Flamingo* (2008), the first in MiPOesias Cuban-American Poetry Series.

"How Do You Say Orange," also appeared in the chapbook *Red Paper Flower* (Little Poem Press, 2004).

"Exilio" and "Granada" were reprinted in *Babel Fruit*.

"My Body as a Communist Country" and "My Body as The Tropicana Nightclub, 1952" were reprinted in *Terrain – A Journal of the Natural & Built Environments*.

JACKLEG PRESS

Brittney Corrigan
Jessica Cuello
Barbara Cully
Suzanne Frischkorn
Victoria Garza
Reginald Gibbons
D.C. Gonzales-Prieto
Neil de la Flor
Caroline Goodwin
Jennifer Harris
Meagan Lehr
Jean McGarry
Jenny Magnus
Rita Mookerjee
cin salach
Maureen Seaton
Kristine Snodgrass
Cornelia Maude Spelman
Peter Stenson
Megan Weiler
David Wesley Williams

jacklegpress.org

CPSIA information can be obtained
at www.ICGtesting.com
Printed in the USA
BVHW070117211022
649943BV00003B/194